the NUMBERS of GOD'S WORLD

1 God made many things that live by the grassy riverbanks of India. **One** cattle egret pecks insects from the back of **one**

large rhinoceros with **one** horn. **One** tiger prowls through the tall grass. Overhead **one** green piper snake dangles from the branch of a tree.

2 God made many things that live in the
hot jungles of Asia. **Two** orangutans
cuddle together. **Two** chameleons cling

to leafy branches. **Two** butterflies flutter in the air.
Two slow lorises play in a tree.

3 God made many things that live in the warm waters of the oceans. **Three** gentle manatees float peacefully among

the drifting green seaweed. **Three** sleek dolphins
swim together. **Three** sea turtles glide through
the water.

4 God made many things that live in a
sunny country field. **Four** small field
mice cling to stalks of tall grass. A herd

of **four** deer listens for danger. **Four** bumblebees buzz among **four** types of wildflowers: bluebells, daisies, thistles, and buttercups.

5 God made many things that live in the clear waters of a coral reef. **Five** starfish cling to a rocky ridge. **Five** copper-banded

butterfly fish swim over **five** colorful tubes of sponge. **Five** sea horses perch on branches of coral.

6 God made many things that live in the grasslands of Africa. **Six** lions rest in the shade of a tree. **Six** ostriches stand at

attention. **Six** meerkats watch the landscape around their burrow.

7

God made many things that live by the calm waters of a pond. **Seven** mallard ducklings swim behind their mother.

Seven lily pads dot the water. **Seven** bright dragon-flies dart through the air. **Seven** cattails wave in the soft breeze.

8 God made many things that live on the American prairie. **Eight** pronghorns roam through the thick grass. **Eight** prairie

dogs play by their underground homes. **Eight** black-eyed susans turn their blooms toward the sun.

9 God made many things that live in the cool north woods of Canada. **Nine** cones grow on the branches of evergreen trees.

Nine flying bats sweep through the air. **Nine** wolves howl in the dusk. **Nine** red mushrooms grow near a rotting log.

10

God made many things that live in cold Antarctica. **Ten** seals rest on a large ice floe. **Ten** birds swoop and